FINISHING LINE PRESS
www.finishinglinepress.com

A Time of Waiting

poems by

Charlotte Melin

Finishing Line Press
Georgetown, Kentucky

A Time of Waiting

ISBN 979-8-89990-431-8 First Edition

ACKNOWLEDGMENTS

With thanks to the online venues where some of the poems in this chapbook appeared:

"After New Year's Eve," *Flying Island*, February 23, 2024.

"Imagine Rain," *Canary*, Issue Number 65 (Summer Solstice Issue), June 20, 2024.

"Summer of Floods," *Tiny Seed Literary Journal* (Water Issue), January 23, 2025.

"Midsummer," *Flying Island*, September 30, 2024.

"Blueberry Picking," *Flying Island*, September 29, 2023.

"Flock," *Flying Island*, July 27, 2022.

"North Shore," *Flying Island*, January 31, 2025.

"Solstice," *Canary* (Winter Solstice Issue), December 21, 2023.

Publisher: Leah Huete de Maines
Editor: Christen Kincaid
Cover Art: Kat Rohn
Author Photo: Matthew Rohn
Cover Design: Elizabeth Maines McCleavy

Order online: www.finishinglinepress.com
also available on amazon.com

Author inquiries and mail orders:
Finishing Line Press
PO Box 1626
Georgetown, Kentucky 40324
USA

Contents

For Matt, Kat, Anne, and Others We Love

After New Year's Eve

Already gone the luminaries
of New Year's Eve that lighted
the curving paths in the park,
the forks to enter or exit.
A chill has settled in,
and silence. A neighbor
lifts the undecorated tree
into his truck, a few kids
straggle over the green.
Here and there a puff
of steam exhales from
a heat vent. At one house
the smell of laundry drifts
over the sidewalk,
reaching out as if we were
all tidying up together.
No one is welcoming
the months to come,
the inevitable discord.
Yet last night in the dark,
the luminaries were so
peaceful as they faintly
flickered promises.

January 6

Pristine as the sun
breaks through—
every branch, twig,
needle turned white
by the ice fog.
Oh, expectation
of miracle
this cold day,
rather than violence.
Each exhalation
becomes visible
in air so bitter it takes
our breath away.

February Sunrise

Stopped to watch sunrise,
its slowness an antidote
to the impatience of
early waking to
yesterday's images—
two deer far off in a field,
a covey of swans browsing
in muddy corn stubble,
at home broken things
in need of repair.
Now, as I wait still,
the sky turns satin
pink, peach, purple,
a contrail crosses the sky
behind silhouetted trees
and I wonder what
more to expect
from the day to come.

Lost Winter

No contrast for
coppered vegetation.
We drove south
then saw snowpack
in the barren woods
and drift remnants
along the highways,
but found mostly
contours thirsty
for water renewal,
this lost winter
worried about
continuing drought.

Imagine Rain

Imagine velvet dark
wakes you with the light
percussive touch of
raindrops and even before
your eyes open, you smell
the earthy scent of moist
dirt, sense the spreading
green of moss,
the push of small leaves
upward that transforms
sweet soil after
a long dry season.
But that rain doesn't come.

Edible Weeds

Khobiza, I read,
mallow,
is an essential
green in Gaza, like
nettles scavenged
across Europe as
armies rake through,
timpsila roots buried
in the prairies—
edible weeds
overlooked until
foraging became
survival.
Every leaf,
root I see now
makes me wonder
what keeps us alive.

Solution Cave

In the cave
the absolute dark
has no gradation,
envelops us
so completely
I hear only
the soft drip of
carbonic acid,
see nothing.
The solution
dissolves karst,
forms stalactites,
stalagmites, flow
stone, ribbons,
unnamed shapes
from mere cracks.
Over millennia,
our guide says,
turning lights on again.
Do not touch,
watch your head
to return to
the external world.

Summer of Floods

This summer we learn
lessons in hydrology—
the continuous
movement of water,
the lateral systems
rain overwhelms,
the way precipitation
far off translates
into weeks of overflow.
Ephemeral streams,
flood pulses, meanders.
How this language
of interconnection
and divergence
teaches patterns
about what little
we control.

Midsummer

After the evening shift
we walked the trail
circling the small lake,
past the pink fireweed to
woods flanked by rocky slopes
covered with blueberries and lichen.
Midsummer in Oslo
and the sky stayed light,
the sun drawing a continuous arc
along the horizon
that curved up after midnight.
As we watched endless day fade
to shadows under the conifers,
the darkest place,
we came face to face
with something that stopped us
in utter silence—
a European elk crossing the path.
All these years later at dawn
when loud warbling fills the trees,
I think about the moment before
the creature vanished,
about the shared dormitory room
that went with the temp job,
the foraging we did thriftily,
about Nixon resigning then
on flickering black-and-white TV
and insurrection hearings now,
about our return flights home to
a country we hoped had changed
into a place where we might find
a lifetime of experiences
filled with love and idealism
rather than turmoil
and be at times speechless
at magic however fleeting.

Blueberry Picking

We needed this day
to remind us of abundance,
of cyclical renewal—
the mixture of sun and clouds,
the air breathable for once,
the wild clematis a white
lace thick with bees.
The drive to the farm leads
up a wooded hill past
wheat fields turned golden,
hollyhocks, mallows, poppies,
the barn where swallows
curl by overhead.
The blueberry picking
is good and children's voices
call out delight to family
in the next row as they
discover the prize.
Afterwards we walk the path
that looks out toward the river,
gleaning more time in this place,
a moment of pause away from
all that troubles this summer—
the smoke and heat and floods.

Gifts

Dark by the time
we got home,
the steamy night
teemed with tree frog
and cicada voices.
Though it was late,
there was basil
to process leaf by leaf
before it oxidized,
precious gift from
a dusk conversation
with old friends that
spun out in drifts
and digressions.
Standing at the sink,
I smelled the pungent
scent on my hands
and carefully set
the fresh peaches
out on the counter
to savor one by one
over the next few days.
U-picked, rare—
each dimpled globe
matchless and redolent.

Flock

Driving home from Indiana
we finally see the blackbirds
I've missed all fall, feeding
in stubbled cornfields. Later
another flock shapeshifts
south in migration, a
mesmerizing murmuration.
We have yet to travel through
the flattest landscape—
past exhausted Streator
and Starved Rock, neither
a refuge for us on the back
and forth to family,
past the distant towers
of the nuclear plant in
Byron, where absent poetry,
tedium turns to thinking
about how decades ago
it seemed that countless
redwings, grackles, starlings
winged overhead and there
was nothing remarkable
about driving mile after mile
as the radio crackled in and out,
no thought of the finitude
of birds, resources, or time.

Migration

It seems impossible that tundra swans
have gathered again by the hundreds
as they migrate down the Mississippi.
Flying in, they hover, land by threes
or more, white against the deep
blue water, graceful and yet ungainly.
Restless ducks intermingle, eagles
fly overhead as the swans call out
to each other, telegraph,
synchronize, vocalize constantly.
We watch the choreography in
awe from the distance while they
pause and momentarily suspend
our thinking. Migrants, migration,
survival. Here, waterfowl feed
on aquatic roots. The river remains
open. Thin ice is forming
on nearby ponds.

North Shore

This beach is all sound,
a crescent bay where
boundaries converge—
birch and balsam,
rhyolite and basalt,
pink stone and water.
Opposite forces
layer the shorescape
in waves and shoulders.
Resonance surrounds.
Listening to it sing,
I try to separate voices
in the cacophony but
hear braided together
the tone of the lake's
liquid muscle and
the timbre of solid rock.
Each tentative step
on such uneven terrain
takes focus and care.
Round stones slide,
tumble perpetually,
crashing surf surges
out of the depths.
Echoes, turbulence
amplify yearning
for profound quiet,
for a walk beyond
our mad divisions
into a vaster space.

Solstice

The solstice waits
like a banked fire—
embers at sunrise,
smoldering sparks
at the sunset end of
a somber afternoon.
What do we look for
in these times,
a light-word
flaring against
the dark? Only
a string of geese
scribbles its way
across the sky.

Growing up in Indiana on the creek-wild cornfield edge of expanding suburbs, **Charlotte Melin** developed an early interest in poetry that has remained a constant in her life. In Indianapolis she met her husband of now fifty plus years, Matthew Rohn, an art historian and professor who has become an environmental activist. She earned a B.A. from Bennington College and a Ph.D. from the University of Michigan. They moved many times for academic jobs before arriving with their family in Northfield, Minnesota in 1994. Over the course of her career as a professor of German studies at the University of Minnesota, she mentored graduate students, chaired her department, collaborated with colleagues across disciplines, and published widely about German poetry, language teaching, and the environmental humanities.

In 2020 as she looked ahead to transitioning into retirement, she knew that among other things she wanted to return to earlier interests in creative writing. The pandemic, of course, changed everything. Daily writing turned into a way to approach what was happening during lockdown—a private form of resistance, a practice of spiritual centering. It meant noticing everyday things, finding words in the midst of social distancing, concentrating on the moment, a pause from jury-rigged meetings on Zoom. Some German poets have conceived of their work as poetry written in dark times against silence, not grand statements but subtly transgressive conversations about trees, like seismographs that register shifts in the world. The writing in the present chapbook tries to be mindful of such potential power of language. The poems are a selection from recent work that has appeared variously online at *Canary, Flying Island, Tiny Seed Literary Journal,* and other venues. Elsewhere she had a longer topographical poem in the Northfield anthology *Bridge and Division* (2023). *A Time of Waiting* is her first published book of poetry.

www.ingramcontent.com/pod-product-compliance
Lightning Source LLC
LaVergne TN
LVHW090543110826
845146LV00003B/1242

* 9 7 9 8 8 9 9 9 0 4 3 1 8 *